True Love

Other Books in Interest from St. Augustine's Press

Josef Seifert, *Christian Philosophy and Free Will*

David K. O'Connor, *Plato's Bedroom:*
Ancient Wisdom and Modern Love

Dietrich von Hildebrand, *The Nature of Love*

Dietrich von Hildebrand, *The Heart:*
An Analysis of Human and Devine Affectivity

Rémi Brague, *On the God of the Christians*
(and on one or two others)

John F. Boyle, *Master Thomas Aquinas & the Fullness of Life*

Max Picard, *The Flight from God*

Marc D. Guerra, *Liberating Logos:*
Pope Benedict XVI's September Speeches

H. S. Gerdil, *The Anti-Emile: Reflections on the Practice of*
Education against the Principles of Rousseau

Edward Feser, *The Last Superstition:*
A Refutation of the New Atheism

Pierre Manent, *Seeing Things Politically*

Leszek Kolakowski, *Religion: If There Is No God . . .*

Jacques Maritain, *Natural Law: Theory & Practice*

Raïssa Maritain, *We Have Been Friends Together &*
Adventures in Grace

Leon Bloy, *The Woman Who Was Poor*

Robert Hugh Benson, *Lord of the World*

Gabriel Marcel, *The Mystery of Being* (in two volumes)

Gabriel Marcel, *Thou Shall Not Die*

Karol Wojtyła [St. John Paul II], *Man in the Field*
of Responsibility

C.S. Lewis and St. Giovanni Calabria, *The Latin Letters*
of C. S. Lewis

True Love

Josef Seifert

ST. AUGUSTINE'S PRESS
South Bend, Indiana

Manufactured in the United States of America

1 2 3 4 5 6   21 29 19 18 17 16 15

Library of Congress Cataloging in Publication Data
Seifert, Josef, 1945–
True love / Josef Seifert. – 1st [edition].
pages cm
Includes index.
ISBN 978-1-58731-889-4 (paperbound: alk. paper)
1. Love. 2. Love – Religious aspects – Catholic Church.
I. Title.
BD436.S435 2014
128'.46–23   2014009626

∞ The paper used in this publication meets the minimum
requirements of the American National Standard for Information
Sciences Permanence of Paper for Printed Materials, ANSI
Z39.481984.

St. Augustine's Press
www.staugustine.net

Cordially dedicated
to all members of my family,
to all my friends and
all persons with whom I am united
in profound and true love
and to all those who long for true love

Contents

Preface by John F. Crosby   ix

True Love   1

Index   55

Preface
by John F. Crosby

Josef Seifert gives us here a brief but deep study of love that is based chiefly on the work of Dietrich von Hildebrand, a neglected phenomenological master. Seifert has a profound understanding of von Hildebrand's thought, including his thought on love. Indeed, I doubt that any living person (apart from Alice von Hildebrand) has as deep a knowledge as Seifert has of von Hildebrand's philosophy. Thus this book, insofar as it is an introduction to von Hildebrand on love, is absolutely reliable.

But not only reliable; Seifert is an important philosopher in his own right. Indeed he is one of the most important European philosophers of his generation. Thus he is able to expand the Hildebrandian account of love by engaging critics whom von Hildebrand did not engage. He engages a significant criticism that comes from existential Thomism, and he engages an even more significant criticism that comes from Anders Nygren in his well-known work on *eros* and *agape*. Nygren famously argued that *agape*, or God's love for us as revealed in Christ, is a love that originates entirely at God's free initiative and that is therefore not responsive to value in human beings; it is a love, Nygren said, that creates value and does not respond to already existing value. Since Seifert (as also von Hildebrand) begins his discourse on love with the claim that love is a response of the lover to the value of the beloved, Nygren's thesis represents a challenge to him. Seifert works through the challenge with nuance, acknowledging all that is undeniably true in Nygren, while preserving and developing all that is undeniably true in the thesis of the responsive character of love.

This little work of Seifert is appearing in the English-speaking world, where the dominant kind of philosophy is not Hildebrandian phenomenology and personalism, but rather analytic philosophy. But Seifert's work will speak to those analytic philosophers who have been working on the question of love, for he deals with the very issues that concern them. Consider one of the most eminent recent studies by an analytic philosopher writing on love: Harry Frankfurt's book, *The Reasons of Love* (Princeton, 2004).

Frankfurt seems to concur with Seifert when he says: "Love is, most centrally, a *disinterested* concern for the existence of what is loved, and for what is good for it. The lover desires that his beloved flourish and not be harmed. . . . For the lover, the condition of his beloved is important in itself, apart from any bearing that it may have on other matters" (42). Seifert aims at just this disinterested concern for the beloved person in all that he says about love as a value-response. Seifert also insists that the lover takes the beloved person as *this individual person,* and so would gladly make his own this from Frankfurt: "The significance to the lover of what he loves is not that his beloved is an instance or an exemplar. Its importance to him is not generic; it is ineluctably particular. For a person who wants simply to help the sick or the poor, it would make perfectly good sense to choose his beneficiaries randomly from among those who are sick or poor enough to qualify. . . . Since he does not really care about any of them as such, they are entirely acceptable substitutes for each other. The situation of a lover is very different. There can be no equivalent substitute for his beloved" (44).

But there is not only concurrence between Frankfurt and Seifert. Frankfurt challenges Seifert's central affirmation about love when he says: "love is not necessarily a response grounded in awareness of the inherent value of its object. . . . It is entirely possible for a person to be caused to love something without noticing its value, or without being at all impressed by its value, or despite recognizing that there really is nothing especially valuable about it" (38). Frankfurt just reinforces his challenge to Seifert when he goes on to say that a parent does not love his children because of their value, but rather finds value in them because he first loves them (40). The reader of Seifert's book will see that Seifert has many intelligent responses to Frankfurt, responses that really engage Frankfurt, and force him to develop, or even abandon, parts of his position. Seifert says in effect to Frankfurt that the very features of love that concern Frankfurt, namely the disinterested character of love and the ineluctable particularity of love, require for their foundation some recognition of love as value-response. But what I especially want to point out is that, though Seifert stands in the phenomenological tradition, he works philosophically in such a way as to have much to say to his analytic colleagues. His book has the potential to open a new and fruitful dialogue between these two philosophical traditions.

TRUE LOVE
Josef Seifert[1]

When we speak in the following of love, we mean primarily the love between persons. Hence, we exclude from our consideration phenomena such as the love of truth, the love of one's country, or the love for Beethoven's late quartets, even though all of these "loves" are not improperly called so but, on the contrary, share many features and possess many important connections with the love of persons.

For much weightier reasons we exclude such a usage of the term "love" as it is found when we say of a Don Giovanni that he loves women, or when we say of an alcoholic that he loves wine. For these acts share with the genuine love for persons only very abstract features, such as a strong affective attachment to something. Yet the "love" of women because of their purely sexual attractiveness or the "love" of wine of the alcoholic lacks even the most basic features of genuine love. We are faced here with radically different phenomena.[2]

The attachment to wine, or to women solely because of their sexual attractiveness, is motivated by the subjective

1   Professor, International Academy of Philosophy-Institute of Philosophy Edith Stein, Granada, Spain.
2   See Dietrich von Hildebrand, *Das Wesen der Liebe,* in D. von Hildebrand, *Gesammelte Werke,* Bd. III, 31–61 (Regensburg-Stuttgart: Habbel/Kohlhammer, 1971). See also D. von Hildebrand, *The Nature of Love,* trans. John Crosby and John Henry Crosby (South Bend, Indiana: St. Augustine's Press, 2009), ch. 1.

pleasure we seek for ourselves. The importance of wine for the alcoholic or of women for Don Giovanni is relative to their subjective satisfaction. The importance of the object here depends completely on our own pleasure.

Love in the sense in which we shall speak of it, on the other hand, is always motivated by a positive importance which is intrinsic to a being—"intrinsic" not only in the sense in which the end possesses intrinsic (i.e., direct) importance, in contradistinction to the means which possess importance only indirectly, borrowing their importance merely from their aptitude to realize a given end. When we speak of "intrinsic importance" in the context of love, we have a radically different phenomenon and sense of "intrinsic" in mind. We mean "intrinsic importance" in the sense of what von Hildebrand has clearly elaborated as "value": i.e., a positive and objective preciousness of a being which is not only an importance for me, relative to my pleasure or even to my objective good. Value is rather an importance which characterizes a being in itself; it could be called an intrinsic preciousness of a being, lifting that being out of the indifferent and neutral in such a way that its goodness cannot be considered to exist only for someone; rather, value characterizes the being which has value objectively. One could say that the beloved being is given as endowed with intrinsic (and positive) importance in two radically different senses. The beloved being is, as Kant and Wojtyła pointed out,[3] to be treated as an end and

3   This corresponds to the famous formulation of Kant's categorical imperative, according to which one should never treat a person, in oneself and in another, as a means solely but always also as an end in itself: "Act always in such manner that you never treat another person solely as a means but always treat the person simultaneously as the end of your action." This version of the

not only as a means.[4] The reason why the beloved being ought to be treated as an end lies in the second sense of intrinsic importance the person possesses, namely, in the fact that the beloved person is endowed with the intrinsic preciousness and dignity of value which differs from any positive importance which exists only for someone.[5]

This call to respect or love a person for his own sake throws further into relief the difference between authentic love and a pseudo-love as Don Giovanni's "love of women." One could say that the object of such a "love" for women or wine attracts us by merely alluring us, leaving us completely masters in the sense that we may or may not

categorical imperative influenced the Polish ethical personalism of the Wojtyła school. See Karol Wojtyła, *Love and Responsibility* (New York, NY: Farrar, Straus, and Giroux, 1982). See also Wojtyła, *Amour et Responsabilité* (Paris, France: Editions du Dialogue/Stock, 1978), 32–6; 27–31, especially 34; "l'essence de l'amour comprend l'affirmation de la valeur de la personne en tant que telle." See also Josef Seifert, "Karol Cardinal Wojtyła (Pope John Paul II) as Philosopher and the Cracow/Lublin School of Philosophy," in *Aletheia*, An International Journal of Philsophy, II (1981), 130–99.

4   Anyone recognizes some intrinsic importance in this sense because no one can exclusively desire means towards ends without desiring some end for its own sake in the sense that it is no longer a means for something else, as Aristotle noted. Pleasure for Don Giovanni is also regarded as an end, although he would never be able to approach a person as an end in himself for the reason given in the text above.

5   See Dietrich von Hildebrand, *Ethics* (Chicago, IL: Franciscan Herald Press, 1972), ch. i–iii. See also Josef Seifert, "Wert und Wertantwort: Hildebrands Beitrag zur Ethik," in *Prima Philosophia*, Sonderheft 1: Ethik (1990); see also Josef Seifert, *Was ist und was motiviert eine sittliche Handlung?* (Salzburg, Austria: Universitätsverlag A. Pustet, 1976); Josef Seifert, *Qué es y qué motiva una acción moral?*, presentación de Alfonso López Qintás, tradd. y ensayo introductorio de Mariano Crespo (Madrid: Centro Universitario Francisco de Vitoria, 1995).

choose to pursue our pleasure—as we like. Our arbitrariness remains unchallenged, so to speak. The object does not address our freedom with a call to respond to it; or at least we are in no way under any sort of obligation to give to the object its due. At the same time, the subjectively satisfying has the tendency to dethrone our freedom, to enslave us. We are confronted here with a seeming paradox: precisely that which leaves our arbitrariness unchallenged has the tendency to dethrone our freedom.

In genuine love, on the other hand, our freedom is neither sidestepped nor dethroned nor is it allowed to remain in a state of "unchallenged arbitrariness." Rather, the being whom we love issues a call addressed to us, even when we are not morally obliged to love another person (e.g., with a special kind of love such as friendship). A beloved being invites and calls us, issues a call to surrender in some sense, or better to give ourselves to the beloved. We no longer remain in a state of arbitrariness, as when we pick and choose among pleasures, but we realize that we ought to love the other person because he or she deserves our love. The philosophers Karol Wojtyła and Tadeusz Styczeń bring out this point beautifully and express it in the principle *persona est affirmanda propter seipsam*, which is according to them the foundational principle of ethics and can be freely translated as: "the person, in virtue of her dignity, ought to be lovingly affirmed for her own sake."[6]

---

6   For the application of the philosophy of intrinsic value and value response, see von Hildebrand, *The Nature of Love*, ch. 1. See also Tadeusz Styczeń, "Zur Frage einer unabhängigen Ethik," in Karol Kardinal Wojtyła, Andrzej Szostek, and Tadeusz Styczeń, *Der Streit um den Menschen: Personaler Anspruch des Sittlichen* (Kevelaer, Germany: Butzon und Bercker, 1979), 111–75; see also T. Styczeń,

Let us turn to another aspect of this: the relation between "love" and its object in the pseudo-love for sex or for wine is one of appropriation or exploitation, one of using an object for the sake of our own pleasure. We remain in a "safe" and complete self-centeredness. This gesture is radically different from the element of abandoning ourselves, of giving ourselves to the other person for her own sake, a gesture which is found in all genuine love. In love we leave the safety of remaining only with ourselves, with our own pleasures and immanent interests. Love audaciously leaves the shore of our own being and crosses the ocean which separates us from another person. The act of love is not only in itself something beautiful and audacious, but it requires audacity also because it renders us vulnerable by making our own life dependent on another person, by binding our own happiness to another's happiness, to his being, to his love, and by making another's unhappiness a source of our own pain.[7]

A further striking difference and even opposition between the two kinds of "love" alluded to consists in the completely different relation the "objects" of these "loves" have to our own pleasure and happiness. In both instances we find some form of "happiness." But in the love for women (sex), money, or wine, this quasi-happiness is only self-centered pleasure, and the object is viewed as a means toward this pleasure. Our pleasure is directly intended as the end; the object of the

"Karol Wojtyła: Philosoph der Freiheit im Dienst der Liebe," in: Karol Wojtyła-Johannes Paul II, *Erziehung zur Liebe* (Stuttgart, Germany: Bernstein, 1979), 155–9.

7 See S. Johannes Hamburger, "Die Kühnheit der Liebe," in: *Wahrheit, Wert und Sein*, ed. B. Schwarz, 90–106 (Regensburg, Germany: Josef Habbel, 1970).

"love" is desired as a mere means. As Wojtyła has shown in beautiful analyses, such a utilitarian approach to love, even if the pleasure is mutual, is destructive of any true communion and love.[8]

Again, there are several attitudes towards other persons which are frequently confused with love—in life as well as in philosophical theories—but which are quite different or even opposed to love.

There is first the possibility of taking towards another person a mere attitude of "using" the other person like a means for a purpose outside the person. All of us need the help of other persons and often "use" other persons to fix our house, to accomplish tasks, etc. But as soon as a utilitarian approach dominates our relation to other persons, as soon as we approach other persons only like means, we depersonalize them, as it were. We approach them like mere things to use. And this attitude is morally wrong as already Kant saw when he formulated the (categorical) moral imperative: "Act always in such manner that you never treat another person solely as a means but always treat the person simultaneously as the end of your action."

Karol Wojtyła—Pope John Paul II—sees in this a formulation of what he calls the personalistic principle upon which morality should rest. He formulates this personalistic principle in the following fashion: "Each time that a person is the object of your act(ion), do not forget that you must never treat him only as a means, as an instrument, but always keep in mind that this person has or at least should have, his own end."

8   See the critique of hedonist theories of love in Wojtyła, *Amour et Responsabilité*, 20–31.

In utilitarianism, a mere using of other persons is coupled with a hedonistic view of the good and a hedonistic approach to other persons. The good is then defined as "the greatest pleasure of the greatest possible number of men." One person's pleasure may actually be—especially in sexual relations—reached by means of another person and yet without hurting the partner. This hedonistic-utilitarian ideal of the good leads to a conception of love according to which one person gets pleasure from the same thing which satisfies another one and this cooperation in providing pleasure for each other and finding it in and through each other would be love. In contradistinction to the case of the rapist or sadist or a Don Giovanni there would be no victim in this kind of combined pleasure-seeking but a common joyful experience.

In an admirable section of his book *Love and Responsibility*, Wojtyła offers a cogent criticism of this hedonistic-utilitarian view of love which may of course easily dominate a marriage or a person's sexual life.

He shows that—as already Aristotle observed—the passing character of pleasure and of its sources renders it likely that the same person who once gave me pleasure ceases to do so in the future. Then my "love" ceases. But how can such a feeling which ceases without any essential change in the beloved person deserve to be called love? This points, as Wojtyła brilliantly observes, to an inner inconsistency in the utilitarian-hedonistic principle "greatest pleasure for the greatest possible number," for it is merely an external, factual bond that links my pleasure to that of another person. Hence, if I only search for subjective pleasure, and if it so happens that the other person's destruction serves my pleasure better than what satisfies him, I will kill or destroy or hurt him as long as I am a strict hedonist. Pleasure as principle has no force to unify persons really, to bridge the gap between them. It is an essentially subjectivist and egoistic principle. The utilitarian principle breaks itself up from within and leads to a "homo homini lupus!"[9]

This points to an even deeper failure of the hedonistic-utilitarian conception of love to do justice to the true nature of love. Even at the time when another human being gives me pleasure he is not being taken seriously as person in his own being, as long as I remain in the utilitarian attitude. He is just used for the sake of my pleasure. (Here the author observes two basic meanings of the Polish word *uzywaz*, which is rendered in French by *se jouir* (*de*): *se jouir de* as "to use" and as "to find pleasure in.") In English this same double meaning is expressed from the side of the means-ends relationship when one speaks of "taking advantage of a woman."

No real communion of persons is possible on this basis of hedonism. Each one remains locked in himself and incapable of transcending to the other. There is not even any real co-experience of pleasure but an isolation and at least a merely exterior arrangement of two egoisms, as Wojtyła puts it. The truly loving person in contrast looks at the beloved being as an end in himself; above all, the reason for his love lies in the other's preciousness, not in his own pleasure.

Moreover, only here do we find true happiness which differs from mere pleasure. This deeper happiness presupposes that we love the other for his own sake. Only if we

9   Hobbes saw in this feature "that one man is to another a wolf" a natural trait of man.

give ourselves in value response to the beloved person for his own sake can this happiness at all be attained, as Scheler, von Hildebrand, Frankl, and others have convincingly shown.

Finally, the difference between the two data called "love" is thrown into relief by the completely different kind of gradation we find in these "loves" themselves as well as in their respective objects. The "love" of wine, of isolated sex, etc., is characterized by degrees of intensity; i.e., the difference between different attractions felt towards purely subjectively satisfying objects is primarily a difference of degrees of intensity. The object of this pseudo-love attracts us more or less in the framework of a quasi-quantitative scale of attractivity. By contrast, in the "more" or "less" of real love, we find, among other things, a hierarchical order of goods reflected. This "more" cannot be reduced to a greater degree of intensity or be interpreted in the light of any quantitative category. Rather, when we compare the love of God with the love of an imperfect man, e.g., we are confronted with a more absolute, more unconditioned, qualitatively different love which responds and corresponds to the higher, nobler, more perfect being of the beloved.

Once we see the fundamental distinction and to a certain extent even opposition between these two types of "love," it also becomes evident that the only phenomenon which really deserves the name love is love as value response. We do not suggest, of course, that love as value response cannot coexist with an attractiveness of the beloved person from the point of view of subjective satisfaction. Even less do we suggest that these two kinds of "love" which we may feel towards another person can merely coexist side by side as two completely separate things. Rather, as can be seen especially in the case of spousal love, the sexual attractiveness of the beloved person can be profoundly formed by, and integrated into, genuine spousal love.[10] Only in its isolated absolutized form is the attraction by the merely subjectively satisfying opposed to authentic love as value response. Once integration, a central category of Wojtyła's philosophical anthropology, has been achieved, all opposition ceases to exist, and the subjectively satisfying, while always remaining different from, and subordinate to, love as value response, becomes formed and transformed by it and plays its legitimate role in love and marriage.

Thus we cannot follow one of Josef Pieper's theses in his noteworthy attempt to overcome the radical split between *eros* and *agape* in Nygren's philosophy and theology of love. Pieper proposes that we proceed in the analysis of love from every datum to which the German word *Liebe* or the English word "love" can refer.[11]

Such an approach presupposes a basic unity of meaning in the term "love." It assumes moreover that,

10 This is a central theme both in Wojtyła's *Love and Responsibility* and in his *opus magnus* that he wrote largely as philosophy professor in Lublin and Cracow but used and published after he had become Pope, in his *Uomo e donna lo creò* (Vatican City: Città Nuova Editrice/Libreria Editrice Vaticana, 1987); *Man and Woman He Created Them: A Theology of the Body*, trans. Michael Waldstein (Boston, MA: Pauline Books, 2006). This great philosophy and theology of the body and of spousal love bears a remarkable similarity to Dietrich von Hildebrand's works, *In Defense of Purity* (London: Sheed and Ward, 1931); *The Mystery of Faithful Love* (Steubenville, OH: Franciscan University of Steubenville Press, 1991); *Man and Woman* (Chicago: Franciscan Herald Press, 1966), and others.

11 See Josef Pieper, *About Love* (Chicago, IL: Franciscan Herald Press, 1974), 1ff.

if there is such a commonality of meaning, it is within this very abstract common element of "love" that the true essence of love can be discovered. It is primarily this latter assumption which we must dispute already on the basis of the above brief investigation. Hence we shall only concentrate on love as value response, on love for other persons which is a response to another person because of his intrinsic worth. This does not exclude the fact that there are aspects and dimensions of love which cannot be reduced to the value-responding gesture of love.

The meaning of "intrinsic worth" or "objective value" is rendered more evident if one considers what von Hildebrand has called the "objective good for the person." This term means a good not insofar as it has an importance in itself (objective value) but insofar as it has importance for someone. In other words, the factor in virtue of which the objective good for the person is lifted out of neutrality, its importance, addresses itself to someone *for* whom it is important. In this respect the objective good for the person resembles the subjectively satisfying. It differs from it decisively, however, in that it is never solely subjectively gratifying but precisely objectively good for the person. It lies in the interest of the true good of the person. It is an objective *bonum mihi, bonum tibi, bonum illi, bonum nobis,* etc.

Perhaps one could say that Aristotle, insofar as he considers happiness (*eudaimonia*) as the end of all human actions, believes that the only motive of love—in the last analysis—is this objective good for the person. Of course, there are passages in which he seems to acknowledge that the friend desires also the good for the friend so that not each person would only be motivated by his own objective good (the *bonum mihi*) but also by the *bonum tibi*.[12] In any case, apart from the incompatibility of such deeper insights with the general thesis of Aristotelian ethics that happiness is the only ultimate end and motive of all human actions, Aristotle does not investigate the radical difference in motivation which is found between my interest in my objective good and the transcending interest in the objective good for the beloved person for his sake, under the point of view that it is an objective good for him. Still less did Aristotle in his famous and beautiful books on friendship consider the difference between being motivated by value as the intrinsic preciousness of a being and by the objective good for somebody.

In his profound analysis of love, von Hildebrand has shown that the interest in another person's happiness for his sake (which Aristotle clearly seems to acknowledge at times) is an even more amazing datum than the interest in intrinsic value and that it can never be deduced from my interest in the objective good and happiness for me. For while the intrinsic value-preciousness of a being is fully objective, and thus universally calls upon everyone to respond to it and to conform himself to it, the objective good for the person has an inevitable subject-directedness. The objective good for someone addresses itself always to the individual center of the person which is radically different in each one of us. Hence to participate in another person's most intimate point of his *Eigenleben*, of his personal life, so as to burn for his happiness under the point of view that something is good for him, is one of the most amazing aspects of the benevolence of love, and one which is most difficult to explain. In Aristotle this

12   See Aristotle, *Nicomachean Ethics*, VIII and IX.

transition from our own ego to the other ego is presented as quite unproblematic and does not lead Aristotle to revise his view that in general each man seeks his own happiness and good. In reality, we find here the new world of benevolence, of *Wohlwollen*, that is not found in pursuing my own happiness.[13] This view that happiness is the end and ultimate motive of all actions has thus two fundamental flaws: first, it completely overlooks value response and the transcending conforming of ourselves to a being because of its intrinsic value preciousness; second, it fails to recognize the two radically different categories of motivation for the objective good of a person—namely, my motivation by my happiness and my motivation by a beloved person's happiness.[14]

---

13 See von Hildebrand, *Das Wesen der Liebe*, ch. 7. See also Robert Spaemann, *Glück und Wohlwollen: Versuch über Ethik* (Stuttgart, Germany: Klett-Cotta, 1990). Fritz Wenisch argued, correctly I think, that this implies that the category of importance of the objective good for myself and of the objective good for another person are two distinct categories of motivation (even though they are, I submit, the same objective category of importance and not another type thereof; I refer here to von Hildebrand's *Ethics*, ch. 7, on the difference between the categories of importance as categories of motivation and as categories of objective importance—properties of being). See Fritz Wenisch, "Self-Regarding and Non-Self-Regarding Actions, and Comments on a Non-Self-Regarding Interest in Another's Good," in *A Journal of Philosophical Inquiry and Discussion: Selected Papers on the Philosophy of Dietrich von Hildebrand, Quaestiones Disputatae* 3, no. 2 (Spring 2013): 10–134.

14 On this point, see von Hildebrand, *Das Wesen der Liebe*, ch. VII, and *Moralia*. See also Josef Seifert, "Dietrich von Hildebrand on Benevolence in Love and Friendship: A Masterful Contribution to Perennial Philosophy," in *Journal of Philosophical Inquiry and Discussion: Selected Papers on the Philosophy of Dietrich von Hildebrand, Quaestiones Disputatae* 3, no. 2 (Spring 2013): 85–106.

We now return, however, to the aspect of love as value response. (We cannot investigate here why love as value response is presupposed for love as "over-value response" in the sense of an interest in another being's happiness for his or her sake.)[15]

Our thesis about love is radical. It seems to go against the clear doctrine of Plato in the *Symposium*, of Aristotle, of St. Thomas, and many others. The thesis is this: as long as another human being or God is desired by us only as the source of our own happiness, we cannot be said to love at all. This does not exclude that both the pleasure and even more the happiness which the beloved person bestows upon us play a role in love and may even co-motivate love in the form of "secondary motives."[16] But as long as another person does not stand before us endowed with a dignity and value which he possesses in himself and as long as we do not respond to him primarily because of his inherent value preciousness, we do not love him at all. This has often been recognized implicitly and in various insights which were not integrated into a whole philosophy of love, and quite clearly by Duns Scotus.[17] In

---

15   This notion of "over-value response" (*Überwertantwort*) is a central addition to Hildebrand's notion of value response, added in *Das Wesen der Liebe*, ch. iiiff.

16   On this notion of happiness as secondary motivating factor, see Seifert, *Was ist und Was motiviert eine sittliche Handlung?*

17   There are passages in Aristotle's books on friendship in which he points out that we love the friend himself for his own sake. So he says in *Nicomachean Ethics* VIII, iii, 1: *kat'hautous philoûsin* ("they love for their own sakes"). Again, in *Nicomachean Ethics* IV, v, 1125 b 32, Aristotle says with respect to the virtue that controls anger that we should feel it towards the right persons, for the right amount of time, etc., all of which factors do not argue from a relation to our nature or strivings, but from the due-principle. Also in St. Thomas's *Quaestiones de caritate*, which deal with Aristotle's

a thoroughgoing manner this value-responding character of love has been seen only in contemporary philosophy.[18]

One could raise a first objection against this view: love precisely differs from what we called value response in that it is precisely not so that the intellectual or other values in the beloved person motivate love. When we say, "I love this girl," we will not be expected to say that we love her because of her superior intelligence or because of her great wit or because she is a wonderful actress. Whereas all of these qualities can be objects of the value response of admiration, love seems precisely to be given to a person regardless of what his or her valuable qualities are. In fact

notion of friendship, this same thought is expressed. Moreover, in his discussion of the love of God, St. Thomas says that this love is more perfect than hope because it is directed to the goodness of God in Himself, whereas hope only sees God as our highest good. Similar thoughts are in his treatises on despair and on hatred of God—the latter being worse because it rejects God not only as our supreme good but as the supreme good as such. Perhaps the strongest and clearest remarks on this are found in Duns Scotus, with some preceding thoughts to the same effect in the discussion of the *affectio justitiae* in Anselm of Canterbury. See on this Josef Seifert, *Essere e persona: Verso una fondazione fenomenologica di una metafisica classica e personalistica* (Milan, Italy: Vita e Pensiero, 1989), ch. ix; Josef Seifert, "A volontade como perfeição pura e a nova concepção não-eudemonística do amor segundo Duns Scotus," in *Veritas*, trans. Roberto Hofmeister Pich (Porto Alegre, Brasilien: Philosophische Fakultät, PUCRS, 2005), 51–84. Cf. also Walter Hoeres, *Der Wille als reine Vollkommenheit nach Duns Scotus* (München: Pustet, 1962).

18 It is chiefly von Hildebrand's merit to have worked out the notion of due-relation and of value response. See his *Ethics*, ch. i–iii, xvii–xviii; his *Wesen der Liebe*, ch. i–v, ix; and his *Moralia* as the three most mature statements of this philosophy of value response, which is found already in his earliest philosophical work, *Die Idee der sittlichen Handlung*, and differentiates his ethics from Max Scheler's, whose notion of *Wertvorzug* is far vaguer.

a girl would rightly become suspicious if we, in declaring our love to her, added: "I love you—because you are so brilliant, so pretty, and such a wonderful actress." Aristotle already makes the similar point that we cannot love a person because he is witty or funny. (We must add that Aristotle made this statement also because he considered the "comical" as one form of the ugly and not as value.)

In reply to this objection we say: it is certainly true that a great wit, even a brilliance of mind or outstanding gift for acting, cannot as such evoke love. But the reason for this fact is not that love is no value response. Rather, the value of the brilliance of mind or of wit is not deeply enough grounded in the being of a person. To possess these values does not make the other person qua person thematic, does not necessarily endow the other being as a whole with preciousness. These values find themselves "on the outside of the person." This leads us to the discovery that love is of course not sufficiently characterized as value response. The value of the person whom we love must be such that it elevates the beloved person as a whole. The value datum in the other person must be "central" so that the values which we perceive in him make him beautiful, noble, good, and loveable as a whole person. Scheler stressed this when he said that love responds to the *individuellen Kern der Dinge, auf den Wertkern* ("to the value-core of things and persons").[19]

Therefore the charm of a person in a deeper sense, the value-radiance of his very being, of his mind, heart,

---

19 Max Scheler, *Wesen und Formen der Sympathie, Gesammelte Werke* Bd. VII (Bern und München: Francke Verlag, 1973), 150ff. See also the English text: Max Scheler, *The Nature of Sympathy*, trans. P. Heath (Hamden, CT: Shoe String Press, 1973), 147ff.

volitional attitudes, is a basis for love. It reveals values which adorn another person as a whole and which are located in the very heart of his being. Also when we are confronted with the depth of a person's mind rather than with his mere brilliance, or with the sensitivity and refinedness of his relation to nature or art, the perception of such qualities of the other person may lead to our love for him, especially the perception of a general value-responding attitude of a person towards the good or towards beauty. The being and value of the person unfolds, in its deepest dimensions, only in the free acts of the person, and no person can be made good without the cooperation of his freedom. Thus the right use of freedom gives a person the deepest personal value, that of moral goodness, in virtue of which alone he deserves to be called a "good person." Moral goodness which proceeds from free stances towards goods and which involves the self-determination of the person lifts up the very being of the person. Moral values alone make the consciously awakened person good qua person, in what is most proper to the person. Intellectual brilliance and any other imaginable gift can never achieve this. Even within the sphere of moral qualities, however, some possess greater beauty than others: mercy more than justice, purity and humility more than honesty, love and kindness more than conscientiousness as professor, etc.

The unique role which free acts play for the constitution of the beauty of a person as a whole does not contradict the fact that we rightly experience the most beautiful dimensions of a person's being as pure gifts both to him and to us. This is no contradiction because freedom is not the opposite of a gift. Freedom does not mean a dimension of a person's being which is autonomously self-sufficient without any influence of anything which does not depend on that person's will. And the gifts which co-constitute the beauty of a person's being do not remain, on their part, outside the sphere of freedom. Rather, freedom unfolds its deepest role in the cooperation with gifts. This can be seen most clearly in reference to love. Love, at least insofar as the discovery of another person's beauty and the feeling of love are concerned, is a pure gift. Yet love is also a free response to the beloved person who has been given to us, and the feeling of love itself allows for, and even requires, the free sanction of our love, the free appropriation and formation of this gift by the use of freedom.[20] And it is precisely love, this synthesis of gift and freedom, which gives the greatest beauty to the loving person and reaffirms always anew the truth of Leonardo da Vinci's word: "A man is as great as his love."

Love presupposes that the beauty of the beloved personality itself becomes transparent to us. Is this really presupposed for any form of love, we could ask? The answer is yes, although the manner of this "becoming transparent" of the value (beauty) of the beloved person as a whole depends very much on the kind, or category, of love. There are enormous differences here between the love of a child, friendship, spousal love, etc.

Now, we have to ask: How does this "becoming

20　See von Hildebrand, *Ethics*, ch. 25. See on the fourfold source of human dignity, which could also be applied to love, Josef Seifert, *The Philosophical Diseases of Medicine and Their Cure: Philosophy and Ethics of Medicine: Philosophy and Medicine, Vol. 1: Foundations* (New York, NY: Springer, 2004); and Josef Seifert, "Dimensionen und Quellen der Menschenwürde," in *Menschenleben–Menschenwürde: Interdisziplinäres Symposium zur Bioethik: Ethik interdisziplinär*, Vol. 3, eds., Hans-Jürgen Kaatsch and Hartmut Kreß (Hamburg/München/London: LIT Verlag, 2003), 51–92.

transparent" of the beauty of a person as a whole occur? Do we get at this beauty simply by a meditation on the ontological essence of each person and on the dignity and high value which flow necessarily from the nature of the person? This is certainly part of the knowledge which precedes love: the discovery of that dignity of the being of the person which distinguishes a person from plants and animals and endows him or her with a unique value called "dignity," the dignity of being a person, the dignity of the human being and nature (the ontological dignity proper to each person). In some types of love, such as parental love for their newborn children or love of neighbor, this form of knowledge of the ontological value of the person stands in the foreground. Yet, in most cases, we discover value-properties in a person which mediate for us the knowledge of this person's individual preciousness and which manifest this preciousness. These concrete valuable properties such as intelligence, depth of mind, moral virtues, and others, play such a mediating role for the perception of the value of the beloved person as a whole in two different ways. They may assume the function of an introduction (von Hildebrand speaks here of an "antiphon") to the preciousness possessed by the beloved person. In other words, the aesthetic values or gifts of a person do not usually constitute exclusively something which he solely has and can lose, however true this is, but they constitute also manifestations of what that person is. In a similar manner, a shared interest for great classical works of music and the dedication of a performing artist to bringing out this beauty of works may allow us not only to admire and cherish these qualities themselves but also constitute an entrance door to the other person himself and his beauty, which discloses itself in and through these precious qualities of his. An ontological-anthropological fact of the activation of the person qua person in and through these characteristics would have to be developed in order to make this dimension and "ground" of love fully intelligible.

The second manner in which the characteristics of a person lead to perceiving his preciousness qua person is even deeper. For the ontological and inalienable dignity which a person possesses is not the deepest value-dimension of a person qua person. It is a value also possessed by Hitler and a demon. Also the preciousness of his individual personality inasmuch as it is disclosed through his talents and other qualities is not yet this deepest value-dimension. Rather, the deepest value and dignity of the person qua person depends on the good use of his freedom and, religiously speaking, on a grace of God which also calls for a free acceptance and cooperation. This is evident when we regard the demonic person. Hence those values of the person which involve the use of freedom and the unique power of self-determination, self-possession, and self-governance of the person constitute the very lovability and dignity of the person in its deepest dimensions. This acquired moral dignity makes the person precious in such a profound way that we even could say that in it alone the ontological dignity and lovability of the person reaches is supreme actualization and perfection. This can also be said, in a different sense, of another, "bestowed," dignity of which the old Catholic mass said that God, who has constituted human dignity in an admirable way, has even more admirably restored it through grace (redemption). Moral goodness alone can make the person capable of free acts good and beautiful as a whole. Moral evil turns the person himself evil and ugly, and in a sense worthy of contempt or hatred.[21] The dignity of the person is thus not only a possession but also the fruit of a constantly renewed "conquest."[22]

That love is a response to another person as a whole in his or her preciousness corresponds also to the fact that the "response" of love is not only the giving of something, of some act in us, but involves a gift of oneself. For only this unique kind of response, self-donation, can do full justice to the person in his or her unique dignity. In his book *Love and Responsibility*, Wojtyła underlines this point with great clarity.[23] In love we find a true self-donation, a giving of one's very being to the other person.

This general feature of love takes on a unique significance in the love of God and in spousal love. In spousal love we find the most perfect human analogue to the full donation of our very own being, of our own intimate life, which occurs in the full sense in man's love for God. In spousal love we make the beloved person in a certain sense the king or queen of our personal life, as von Hildebrand has elaborated in his book on love.[24] This kind of self-donation is different from the one present in the love of neighbor or of an enemy, where we love the other person

---

21 Those of us who are Catholics or other Christians, who do not hold a predestination to hell independently of free will, believe that every man, as long as he lives on earth, retains a fundamental loveableness. But if he were to turn evil eternally, this loveableness would be absorbed by the evil in him, although even in the demon remains some ontological value that makes him loveable as endowed with a sublime ontological dignity and therefore the fall of the demon deserves our lamentation that God in Ezekiel 28:12–17 demands from the prophet.

22 This is an insight of Gabriel Marcel that to be a person is not just a possession but a conquest (*être personne n'est pas une possession, mais une conquête*).

23 See *Love and Responsibility*, ch. 1.

24 *Das Wesen der Liebe*, ch. iii; vii–ix; xi.

with a kindness or mercy in which we "step outside" and forget, as it were, our own personal life and happiness. In these other kinds of love we leave the domain of our own personal happiness and intimacy. In spousal love, however, the self-donation is precisely the donation of our own being in its most personal and intimate life.

In a magnificent section of his book *Love and Responsibility*,[25] the author speaks about the mysterious paradox which lies in this self-donation of the person in love. For in one sense it is true that the person is absolutely inalienable and cannot give himself away like a possession or like a thing. He must not, and ultimately never can, abrogate his autonomy, or his freedom and responsibility, in order to be some other person's possession or follow his directions in complete blindness.[26] The author of *Love and Responsibility* expresses the feature of self-donation in love, as uniquely present in spousal love, in the following way:

> Spousal love differs from all the other . . . forms of love which we have analyzed. It consists in the gift of the person. Its essence is the gift of one's self, of one's own "I." . . . We find here something which is at the same time different from, and more than, . . . even benevolence. All these (other) manners of coming out of oneself in order to go

25 Ibid., Ch. 1.
26 Again, in another sense, as we believe as Christians, the human person belongs as creature only to God the Creator and the Redeemer. And yet it is true that not only to God in a unique manner but also to another human being man gives himself, and belongs to, in love. The fact that in spousal love and in its consummation in marriage we belong so completely to another creature calls even specially for a divine permission and consecration of marriage.

towards another person go less far than spousal love. "To give oneself" is more than being kindly disposed towards someone and wishing him well, even in the case where, due to (the intensity of) our will for the other's good, another "I" becomes in some fashion "mine" (another self) as this takes place in friendship. . . .

(Yet) first the question poses itself whether one person can give himself to another one, since . . . each person is by his very essence inalienable and *alteri incommunicabilis*. Hence the person . . . can neither alienate himself from himself nor give himself away. The nature of the person opposes itself to the gift of oneself. . . . The person as such cannot like a thing be owned by another one. Consequently, it is equally excluded to be permitted (able) to treat the person like a (mere) means for our own pleasure. . . . But in the order of love and in a moral sense (the gift of oneself) can take place. Here one person can give himself to another one—to man or to God—and thanks to this gift a particular form of love comes into existence which we shall call spousal love. This fact proves the dynamism peculiar to the person and the proper laws which govern the existence and development of the person. Christ has expressed this in the following word which can appear paradoxical: "Whosoever shall find his life, shall lose it, and who will lose his life for my sake, shall find it.". . . Thus the most complete love expresses itself precisely in the gift of oneself, in the fact of the gift of this inalienable and incommunicable

"I." The paradox here is two-fold and goes in two directions. First, (it consists in the fact) that one is capable to come out of (and leave behind) one's own self. (In the order of nature, the person is ordained toward self-perfection.) And secondly (it consists in) that, in doing so, one neither destroys nor devalues it (the "I") but on the contrary develops and enriches it. . . .

Spousal love can never be fragmentary or accidental in the interior life of the person. It constitutes always a particular crystallization of the whole human "I" (self), who, thanks to his love (freely) decides to dispose of himself in this manner. In the gift of oneself, we find therefore a striking proof of self-possession.[27]

One could say that love, because it responds to the other person as whole, and to the extent to which it involves self-donation, is at the same time "more than a value response" and a value response in the fullest sense in that only love can fully give to another person the response which is due to him.

Does true love not often love the less perfect person more than the more perfect one? Do we not love him because he is "himself" and not because of any values?

The whole concept of love being a value response and the interpretation of the self-donation found in spousal love as a response due to another person in virtue of his

27   Wojtyła, *Love and Responsibility*, Ch. 1.

intrinsic preciousness could be objected to on other grounds. One could point out some important facts. We often love a person more who is morally less noble than another one. And when we love a person, especially with spousal love, we will never say that we love him for the sake of his justice, his kindness, etc., but for his own sake. Scheler has especially emphasized this point. So has Pieper. We would agree with these thinkers (without denying that a very silly, superficial, or mean person would not awaken our natural love). Thus the facts alluded to in this objection must be admitted.

The answer to the raised difficulty first requires that we see that love does indeed never respond merely to qualities of the person, not even to virtues and gifts as such, however deeply they affect the very being of their bearer. Love responds to the other person as a whole, or to the person simply speaking. We love another person, not his virtues and qualities. Yet the attractive and good qualities—and this applies particularly to the moral virtues—of a person are not attached to the being of a person in an exterior fashion. Rather, in and through the values in the person the value of the very being of the other person reveals itself to us and is objectively actualized. Aristotle makes a remark in this sense.[28] Aristotle refers there, among other things, to the fact that the friend as a whole is found noble and loveable.

Furthermore, the fact cannot be denied that we often love a person of lesser moral stature more than the better one. Thus our previous remarks about moral goodness having a greater share than other qualities of the person in the constitution of the value and beauty of the person as a

28   *Nicomachean Ethics* VIII, iii, 1. Cf. also ibid., VIII, ii, 5.

whole should not be misconstrued so as to exclude that other gifts, talents, and qualities are presupposed for the loveableness of a person. Many of these qualities are pure gifts for which a human being is neither positively nor negatively responsible. Natural endowments and gifts of the human person co-constitute his being and essence: a fine mind, a strong will, a great vitality, a beautiful physical appearance.[29] Nevertheless, it seems true to say that all of these pure gifts could not by themselves suffice to evoke true personal love without any values which are dependent on the use of the freedom of a person and which involve the free cooperation with gifts or at least the absence of a refusal by the will of these gifts. Even when we love a person who is incapable of actualizing at the present moral values (the infant), even when many love a person who is morally corrupt, when parents love a child who is quite unnaturally evil, their love will anticipate future moral goodness or presuppose that "deep down" and ultimately the beloved person is also morally good. Were one to suspect a total absence of present or future moral goodness in another person and believe him to be demonic, one could no longer love him except inasmuch as the mourning of his fall would still be a sign of love for the person in his original beauty. Should somebody fail to believe that a demonic person beyond the possibility of moral improvement is possible, he may deny that the described case ever occurs but could still grant that if there are demonic and permanently evil persons, these can no longer be loved, precisely because love always embraces another person also in such aspects of his dignity and value which can only be

---

29 Moreover, the Christian believes that the most ennobling quality, grace, is a pure gift.

actualized through free moral goodness, which does not exclude that a loving pain over the loss of a soul or of an angel still entails elements of love even for a demon.[30]

Do we love values rather than persons? Love and free will.

Another objection to calling love a value response is the following: the expression sounds as if we were not to love the other person but rather something which he possesses and bears: his value.

Certainly, it is true that we do not love the value(s)

---

30 Look at this astonishingly beautiful description of the original beauty of Lucifer in Paradise from Ezekiel and the moving exhortation of God to us that we ought to lament the fall of such a great angel (which shows how God loves forever the beautiful angel Lucifer as He created and intended him): "Son of man, take up a lamentation for the king of Tyre, and say to him, 'Thus says the Lord GOD, You were the seal of perfection, full of wisdom and perfect in beauty. You were in Eden, the garden of God; every precious stone was your covering: the sardius, topaz, and diamond, beryl, onyx, and jasper, sapphire, turquoise, and emerald with gold. The workmanship of your timbrets and pipes was prepared for you on the day you were created. You were the anointed cherub who covers; I established you; you were on the holy mountain of God; you walked back and forth in the midst of fiery stones. You were perfect in your ways from the day you were created, till iniquity was found in you. By the abundance of your trading you became filled with violence within, and you sinned; therefore I cast you as a profane thing out of the mountain of God; and I destroyed you, O covering cherub, from the midst of the fiery stones. Your heart was lifted up because of your beauty; you corrupted your wisdom for the sake of your splendor; I cast you to the ground, I laid you before kings, that they might gaze at you. . . .'" (Ezekiel 28:12–17).

of the beloved person but the beloved person himself. In this sense, we could say and admit frankly that love strictly speaking is not a value response but a response to a being (person). As Marcel would put it, we must see a preciousness of what the other person is, not only of what he has, in order to love him. For this reason the profoundest level of values which motivate love are either those which are ontologically inseparable from the very being of a person, or—and this is at least of equal importance—those which presuppose a person's use of freedom: moral and religious values. For here we are confronted with the love of truth of a person, with his justice or wisdom—and for these virtues man is responsible; he has to cooperate for them to exist. They proceed from his free center, and this free center of the person constitutes in a sense the core of uniqueness in the person. Hence the values which reside at this free core of the person adorn him with a goodness which is far from being restricted to something which he merely has; they lift up his very being.[31]

Thus we may conclude that love is indeed a value response, but one which does not only presuppose that we grasp some quality of the person as intrinsically precious, but rather that we grasp the being of another person as a whole and in its very depth as precious. It presupposes that the beauty of the beloved personality itself becomes transparent to us—in very different manners depending on the category of love—through the beloved person's value-bearing qualities. And this will most readily occur in those values which involve the use of freedom and the

---

31 On this, see von Hildebrand, *Ethics*, ch. xxv, on "cooperative freedom."

unique power of self-determination, self-possession, and self-governance of the person.[32]

Scheler insists on this point too when he stresses that love responds to the unique and irreplaceable being which the other himself is, not to something "of him" or "in him."[33] Von Hildebrand makes the same point.[34] Nevertheless, this concession has not yet been fully integrated in the value philosophy of love.

Of course, the phrase "value response" was never meant to exclude that the response is really given to a good, i.e., not to a value but to a being endowed with value and unified by value; the thesis that love is a value response was never intended to deny that we love a person in his intrinsic preciousness. The phrase "value response" (introduced by von Hildebrand) as applied to love meant primarily that we love the other person because he possesses intrinsic preciousness and value. This value-preciousness is in no way attached to a being from without; it is not even just given to him. The value-preciousness is rather a true property of the other person's being and inseparable from it: it resides at the very core of his being.

Mark Roberts, my former student, later a professor at

---

32 These terms are used in Karol Wojtyła, *The Acting Person* (Boston, MA: Reidel, 1979); cf. also the corrected text, authorized by the author (unpublished), Library of the International Academy of Philosophy/Instituto de Filosofía Edith Stein, Granada, Spain.

33 Scheler, *Wesen und Formen der Sympathie, Gesammelte Werke* Bd. VII (Bern und München: Francke Verlag, 1973), 6th edition, pp. 150 ff., esp. 168. See also the English text: Scheler, *The Nature of Sympathy* (Anchor Books), transl. P. Heath, introd. W. Stark (Hamden, Connecticut: Shoe String Press, 1973), 147ff.

34 See von Hildebrand, *Ethics*, ch. i–iii; xvii–xviii; *Das Wesen der Liebe*, ch. iv–xi.

the University of Rhode Island and now a professor at the Franciscan University of Steubenville, has made the profound objection that this close union between value and being does not do away with the distinction between a being and its value, if we want to avoid the mistake of the "naturalistic fallacy." Hence the expression "value response" as applied to love is really literally untrue and also potentially misleading because we do not in fact love a person's value but his being. I agree with this objection and therefore do not think that one ought to say simply and literally that love is a value response. We should seek for a simple and more adequate term. Nevertheless, as long as we have not found a better term, we can expand the notion of value response so far that any response to a being insofar as it is endowed with intrinsic value is called value response; and this wider and less precise meaning of the phrase "value response" was at stake when the term was used, especially by von Hildebrand, who always insisted that we love the person for his own sake and not for the sake of a value separated or separable from him. It is truly and primarily insofar as the beloved person is intrinsically precious that we love him. Understood in this sense, it is not only adequate language which is being used, but it was a profound philosophical discovery which has led to the designation of love as value response.[35]

A further objection against love as value response can be raised in the light of an essential trait of love which Scheler especially stresses: when we love a person,

---

35   See Josef Seifert, „Being and Value. Thoughts on the Reform of the Metaphysics of Good within Value Philosophy" in *Aletheia* I, 2 (1977) (German and English).

particularly when we are "in love" with a person, we are usually unable to give our reasons why we love.[36] This notorious inability to formulate the reasons for our love proves seemingly that love, at least spousal love, is no value response. For in (other) value responses, like admiration, esteem, etc., we are usually pretty well able to state the reasons for them, while love seems inexplicable and mysterious.[37]

In response to this objection, notice that there are simply not enough concepts and linguistic expressions to formulate all of the general value-qualities which we perceive, even as there are also not enough words to express all color-shades and hues. This incapacity to express in words all perceived differences does not only afflict the ordinary man; not even the poet can, as Ingarden has shown, express all nuances of values. There are infinitely many "indeterminacy spots" in each literary work of art where the reader and more clearly the actor have partially to "fill in" (concretize) what the poet left undetermined.[38] Besides, the value in virtue of which we love a person is too individual for it to be classified at all. There is no general value quality which could sufficiently explain why we love a given person, for the value at stake is inseparable from his individual being—from the irreplaceable being of his "thou." In this sense the ultimate reply to the question why we love a person is the one Pieper and Scheler give: "because thou art thou."[39]

In addition, not every person is equally called to give

36　See Scheler, *Wesen und Formen der Sympathie*, 152.
37　See ibid., 147ff., especially 151.
38　Roman Ingarden, *The Literary Work of Art: An Investigation on the Borderlines of Ontology, Logic, and Theory of Literature* (Evanston, IL: Northwestern University Press, 1973).
39　Scheler, *Wesen und Formen der Sympathie*, 163, 168.

a certain value response and especially to love. For the reason of love does not only lie in the beloved person but also in the mysterious moment of an "akinness" of soul, an ordination and affinity between persons, an important factor in love to which Violaine's words in Claudel's *Annonce Faite à Marie* refer: "Il y a un grand mystère entre nous."[40]

Finally, love, especially spousal love, does not always prefer the better person, and is thus not only a response to value because it involves also a mystery of mutual affinity and decision for the beloved person which cannot simply be explained as being called for by the beloved person, and which originates in the mystery between two persons and in the mysterious recesses and spontaneity of the free center of a person.

Although all of this is true, the preciousness of an individual person as a whole is "nourished," "supported by," and "lives on" certain values and qualities which can be referred to by means of general concepts, albeit quite imperfectly: we will say of our love for our child that we love our daughter more than a dog because of the dignity and preciousness of a person, the ontological value of the person which is deserving of love and which the dog lacks. We will in some limited and yet important sense say of our friend or spouse that we love him or her because she or he has such a fine mind, such a great compassion, such a profound understanding of art or of other persons, etc.[41] Against Scheler or Pieper I would insist on the fact

---

40 Paul Claudel, *Annonce Faite à Marie*, Act II.
41 In art, this finds a wonderful expression in the love scene between Othello and Desdemona in the second scene of Verdi's *Othello*.
42 Scheler, *Wesen und Formen der Sympathie*, 152–63, especially 168. Cf. Pieper, *About Love*, 24ff.

that we do not betray love but make only incomplete statements when we make such assertions.[42]

One should also emphasize that the reason for love which can be formulated—"because you are you"— should not be misinterpreted. There certainly is a core of the being of a person which retains an ontological value as long as the person exists and is himself, even if he were a demon. But this cannot be a sufficient reason for love. There is another "core of preciousness" in each human person as long as he lives and can still change and improve. This preciousness as such suffices to ground a pure love of our neighbor or of our enemy but not friendship, spousal love, etc. In these latter types of love the preciousness which is linked to the fact that the other person is this unique person is insufficient in itself to motivate love. Only when this value is united with other sources of value in the person which are not intrinsically inseparable from a contingent person can we love him as friend or as spouse. Otherwise we confuse the logos of spousal love or friendship with that of love of neighbor; some disastrous consequences of this confusion can be seen in Prince Myshkin's love for Nastassya Filipovna in Dostoyevsky's *The Idiot*.

Is the inner value and beauty of the beloved an effect of love rather than its reason?

It has also been said that the beauty and value which we perceive in a beloved person is not the reason for our love but its result. Only because we love do we come to see the

43 These are distinguished by von Hildebrand in his *Das Wesen der Liebe*, ch. i.

other person as precious. This statement can be understood in different ways.[43]

First, love could be presupposed in order for us to see a beauty which the beloved person objectively possesses. It is undoubtedly true that the loving person perceives a beauty which the "sober" man will not perceive. But this is no valid objection to the value-responding character of love. For it could be true that love, in order to come into being, already presupposes a first perception of the beauty of another person as a whole. This is certainly the case. But once we love, we perceive the beauty of another person far better and more deeply. Love opens our eyes for the other person, for his beauty. Love leads to further knowledge which in turn may enhance greater love. Thus there is an endless dialectic between knowledge rendering love possible and love permitting deeper knowledge. Augustine, Pascal, Goethe, Scheler, Hildebrand, and many others have seen this.[44]

A second way to understand the priority of love over the perception of beauty is the conception that the beauty

44 See especially von Hildebrand, *Sittlichkeit und ethische Werterkenntnis, in Jahrbuch für Philosophie und phänomenologische Forschung*, Bd. V (Halle A.D.S.: Niemeyer, 1922). ; Sittlichkeit und ethische Werterkenntnis. Eine Untersuchung über ethische Strukturprobleme. Habilitationsschrift. (München: Bruckmann, 1918), in: Jahrbuch für Philosophie und phänomenologische Forschung, volume 5. Halle: Niemeyer. 1922.pp. 462–602. Sonderdruck der Habilitationsschrift, ebd. 1921. Reprint Vols. 3–6 (1916–1923) 1989. Bad Feilnbach 2: Schmidt Periodicals; 2nd ed. (unaltered reprint, together with Dietrich von Hildebrand, Die Idee der sittlichen Handlung), Dietrich-von-Hildebrand-Gesellschaft (ed.), (Darmstadt: Wissenschaftliche Buchgesellschaft, 1969), pp. 126–266; 3., revised posthumous edition (Vallendar-Schönstatt: Patris Verlag, 1982); Moralidad y conocimiento ético de los valores [presentación y traducción Juan Miguel Palacios], Madrid: Cristiandad, 2006).

of the beloved is a mirage, an illusion created by love. E. T. A. Hoffmann in the Kater Murr, the "Zaubertrank" in Goethe's *Faust* (*Mit diesem Trank im Leibe sieht er gleich Helenen in jedem Weibe*), Freud's notion of the sublimation of libido generating love, and Nietzsche's genealogy of morals suggest this. Now it is unquestionably the case that many attitudes accompanying love often lead to an illusion of a non-existent beauty in the beloved person. The pride of parents lets them believe their children are the most beautiful, intelligent, etc. The sexual desire in a man or woman who are not debased enough to admit to themselves that they want nothing but sexual pleasure may produce such illusionary imagined beauty in another person. For persons of some nobility only want to marry another person and sanction the actualization of their sexual life when they truly love another person or at least respect him. Thus their half-conscious sexual attraction by another person may lead them to adorn him with an imaginary preciousness. It may also be an inordinate desire for happiness which motivates a man or woman to claim that his or her beloved is the most noble and beautiful on earth.

Or again, it may be a general naiveté which makes someone believe that a very pretty girl must be an angel. It may also be a disordered and irrational element in a love which leads to blindness by overextending the "credit" which each true love gives to the beloved. The person who truly loves believes and hopes that the person who is loved by him is good or acted in a good and beautiful way; the loving person will believe this as long as he has no counter-evidence which unambiguously refutes this belief. Such a "credit" to the beloved which is one of the greatest gifts genuine love gives, may, however, in an inordinate or irrational manner, be extended to the beloved person in a passionate, stubborn, irrational, or even foolish way; such defects in the credit of love may have their origin in various imperfections of the character of the loving person.

All of the attitudes, which factually often accompany love, or the disordered love itself, may indeed make a person blind and create illusions. Yet, nevertheless, the proverb "love makes blind" is still untrue when it is meant as referring to the essence of true love. For authentic love is radically different from the described attitudes. True love only wants to see the beauty which is really found in the beloved person—actually or potentially. True love sees both of these but distinguishes between that beauty of the "true self" of the other person which is yet a mere promise or a vocation, and the beauty which he already actually possesses. The person who truly loves sees the faults and deficiencies of the beloved far more clearly and is pained over them more deeply than any person who takes a non-loving attitude.

Thirdly, the priority of love over beauty could be interpreted in an ontological sense. It could be meant that love creates not illusionary but real beauty in the beloved person. Regarding this thesis, various remarks are needed and various interpretations possible.

It is certainly correct to say that love plays a tremendous role in education and in the improvement of persons. It gives to the person who is being loved a spiritual "home" and "shelteredness"; it extends to him a credit of trust which inspires a positive self-confidence and goodness. Above all, it holds out to him the image of his own better self, of his vocation, so to speak. In this sense, love is indeed creative in contributing to make the beloved person better, as Scheler especially noticed,[45] not without the free cooperation of the beloved person, however.

It should not be denied either that there is one value which is the direct consequence of the fact that a being is loved. Saint Exupéry brings out this point very beautifully in *Le Petit Prince*, especially in the description of the en-counter between the little prince and the fox and in the role the act of "taming" (*apprivoiser*) plays in the ensuing part of the story. This *apprivoiser* must be interpreted as the act or deed of love in virtue of which the beloved being is endowed with a unique preciousness which he receives as a result of being loved. It is the value the beloved being possesses qua loved which is at stake here. Although this point seems to be exaggerated in *Le Petit Prince* so as to almost suggest that a being possesses no unique value prior to being loved, it cannot be denied that "to be loved" always involves that a new value of being loved and of attaining thereby a new dignity is bestowed upon the beloved being, at least as far as finite beings are concerned. This may be most evident when an animal is loved by a person or when we contemplate the dignity human persons receive by being loved by God.

Is love not a response to the being (esse) of the person rather than to his values?

This fact leads to another related and quite radical objec-tion which could be raised against the conception of love as a value response. Existentialist Thomists could say:

45   See Scheler, *Sympathiegefühle*, 156–57, 162.

love quite obviously does not respond to the value of a person but to his real existence. For we do not love even the noblest characters in plays, such as Cordelia in *King Lear*—at least not in the sense in which we love a real person, however imperfect he may be from a moral point of view.

From this correct observation some Thomists have drawn the conclusion that it is really the existence of the beloved person which is the primary motivating ground of love. Thomas Aquinas calls existence the perfection of all perfections (*perfectio perfectionum*). Pieper interprets this and applies it to love when he says that the most beautiful thing a being can do is to exist. Thus love seems to respond not to the value but to the existence of the beloved person.[46]

In reply to this objection the following can be said. First, when we spoke of values as motivating love, we did not refer to something outside the order of real being; we did not mean an ideally existing sphere of values. Certainly, as an "incorrigible" Platonist, I would assert the ideal existence of values or of "value-eide" and value-ideas. I would even hold that the philosopher can have a certain deep "love" of this world of immutable "value-eide," of an immutable order of essences of values.[47] But the intrinsic value and preciousness of the beloved person is not—as Rickert, N. Hartmann, and even Scheler

---

46 See Pieper, *About Love*, 24–5.
47 See Josef Seifert, "Essence and Existence: A New Foundation of Classical Metaphysics on the Basis of 'Phenomenological Realism,' and a Critical Investigation of 'Existentialist Thomism'", *Aletheia* I (1977), 17–157, 371–459, especially ch. I, 5; more extensively in Josef Seifert, *Sein und Wesen/Being and Essence* (Heidelberg: Universitätsverlag C. Winter, 1996), ch. 1.

at times suggest—something which is divorced from reality like a star above and outside the real world. No, while there are ideal "value-eide," values can be fully real as the real intrinsic preciousness of real beings. Being-as-valuable constitutes even the innermost dimension or meaning of being. In their inseparable union with the being which bears them, real values characterize and permeate real beings as their real and inmost preciousness.[48]

Secondly, we may grant to the objection that it brings up a very important point which value-philosophers have rarely recognized and only recently stated in a systematic way.[49] Love is not sufficiently and perhaps not even quite adequately described as value response. This is so not only because one loves a person in his value; one does not love his value as such. It is also so because love responds to the other person qua existing, not only "qua possessing intrinsic preciousness." Even the noblest character as a mere possibility or fiction could not motivate real love; we can "love" Shakespeare's Cordelia (*King Lear*) or Dante's Beatrice (*Divine Comedy*) only in a purely analogous sense. Existence which is indeed in a sense *perfectio perfectionum* posits all perfections in reality. Karol Wojtyła brings this point out forcefully in *The Acting Person* when he states that the human person, who must be interpreted in the light of his free act(ion) in which he actualizes his being in a unique way, must never be severed from the

---

48 See on this John F. Crosby, "The Idea of Value and the Reform of the Traditional Metaphysics of Bonum," in *Aletheia* I (1977), 231–339. See also Josef Seifert, "Being and Value: Thoughts on the Reform of the Metaphysics of Good Within Value Philosophy," in *Aletheia* I (1977), 328–36.
49 See also Seifert, Essere e Persona, ch. v–vii; and Seifert, *Sein und Wesen*, ch. 5–7.

ontological foundation of all of his acts and actions: "We find that all acting presupposes the real existence of the agent. Existence lies at the origin of everything that is in man. . . . Coming into being is the 'first act' of every being and only because he is a being can man become the subject of acting. This strict relationship between acting and existing allows us to subscribe to the traditional principle, 'for something to act, it must first exist.'"[50]

Not dwelling here anymore on Wojtyła's profound philosophy of person and existence, of free acts as "enactment of existence," or on his philosophy of the substantial uniqueness of the person, we wish to stress here only that the philosophical conception of value response, of which Wojtyła as philosopher is one of the most forceful defenders, is fully linked in his work with the insight into the absolutely crucial role of existence for the being of the person and for love. It is indeed the attitude of the lover to wonder at the existence of the beloved person and to say to him: how wonderful that you exist! To have stated this clearly is an important philosophical contribution in J. Pieper's book *About Love*.[51]

Thirdly, the objection Thomists might raise against the notion of love as value response requires the following answer. If we simply say (without immediate further differentiation) that existence is the most beautiful thing the beloved person can do, we forget that his being is equally constituted by his essence, not only by his existence. Both of these "principles of being" are absolutely decisive for the constitution of the "loveableness" of a being—albeit in a very different sense. When we love, it is extremely

50   *Esse praecedit agere.*
51   Ibid., 24ff.

important for us *what* the beloved being is (that he is a person rather than a frog or a mouse), *who* he is (that he is this ineffable individual person rather than someone else), and *how* he is (that he has got this individual personality, is good, faithful, etc.) All of these dimensions of the being of a beloved person—his what, who, and how—are, however, aspects of his essence. Hence, only in a certain and limited sense is it true that for love the existence of the beloved person has a priority over his essence; this is true insofar as it is in virtue of his existence only that anything "in him," that he himself is placed in reality. In another sense the essence of the beloved person is more decisive for love than his existence.

Would existence be given, but instead of the existence of the beloved person that of a frog or of a stone, love would be made impossible. Thus we may say that in love we respond in a unique and profound fashion to both the being (existence) of the beloved person and rejoice in that the beloved person exists, and to his essence, rejoicing over that it is he, a person, and *this person*, who exists. It is ultimately he, his very being as this person, whom we love. And the beloved being is neither reducible to his existence nor to his essence; he is rather the unspeakable union of both, this unique personal being which transcends both essence and existence as a tertium.[52] It is he whom we love and whose preciousness is constituted both by his essence and by his existence.

Fourthly, we could say: it is clear that in many cases a love is primarily inspired by the essence of a being, even when

52 Here I presuppose a metaphysical knowledge of the relationship between essence and existence, which I have expressed in *Essence and Existence*, ch. ii–v, , and more extensively in Sein und Wesen (KURSIV).

this essence is conceived as mere possibility, not by existence. The love of a being in view of its essence (possibility) may even motivate the creative act of bestowing existence upon that being. Thus the artist conceives in his mind of many possible works and he decides to bring into existence the one creation which he loves most because of its nature. Similarly, one could think here of parents who have an anticipatory love for children even before they are conceived. One can fathom that the divine Creator finds a (partial) reason for bestowing existence on his creatures in the goodness and beauty of their essence contemplated as idea from eternity.[53]

Fifthly, in the discussion of the Thomistic emphasis on existence of a person as the most profound reason for loving him, we must not forget a truth which Scheler emphasizes especially and which helps to shed light on the perfect compatibility between love as value response and the Thomistic emphasis on the existence of the beloved person. Provided that the nature of a being is good and bears values, the existence of such a good is itself bearer of a unique "existential value." Not only can all values come to really exist in a being but existence of a good is itself bearer of a unique and profound value. Thus the word of love "how good that you exist" has itself the character of a value response; this insight should suffice to dissipate the last remainders of the false semblance that the conception of love as value response is in any way opposed to the Thomistic insight into the crucial role of existence (*esse*).

---

53 St. Beda the Priest has expressed this in profound texts which show a new and in a certain way stronger Platonism—which also assumes individual divine ideas of each person—in Christian philosophy.

Is only **eros**-*love a value response and* **agape**-*love not at all?*

A further objection could be raised against love being a value response. This objection has been most forcefully (and perhaps also most one-sidedly) advanced by Nygren.[54] Only *eros*, says Nygren, is motivated by values. *Agape*, which alone is love in the truest sense, is not motivated by any values. It gives itself freely to beings which are not deserving of this love in virtue of any preciousness or value they have. We have only to think of the marvelous description of mercy by Portia in Shakespeare's *The Merchant of Venice*[55] or in his *Measure for Measure* in order to see this. On the natural plane, this is exemplified by the love of parents for their children in the case in which the

---

54 Pieper, *About Love*, 24–5.
55 William Shakespeare, *The Merchant of Venice*, Act IV, Scene 1:
    PORTIA: The quality of mercy is not strain'd,
    It droppeth as the gentle rain from heaven
    Upon the place beneath: it is twice blest;
    It blesseth him that gives and him that takes:
    Tis mightiest in the mightiest: it becomes
    The throned monarch better than his crown;
    His sceptre shows the force of temporal power,
    The attribute to awe and majesty,
    Wherein doth sit the dread and fear of kings;
    But mercy is above this sceptred sway;
    It is enthroned in the hearts of kings,
    It is an attribute to God himself;
    And earthly power doth then show likest God's
    When mercy seasons justice. Therefore, Jew,
    Though justice be thy plea, consider this,
    That, in the course of justice, none of us
    Should see salvation: we do pray for mercy;
    And that same prayer doth teach us all to render
    The deeds of mercy.

latter are perverted. Nygren points, however, to the divine love for creatures in order to make his point. He proceeds to ascribing this love (*agape*), which is, according to him, independent from all motivation by values, also to man's love of God. Although Nygren is primarily a theologian, his theory raises an objection against the philosophical position that love is essentially a value response—for the datum of *agape*-love, as it is undoubtedly found in the lives of Christian saints, can also be investigated by the philosopher so far as its experienced content and motivation are concerned. And, as even Bergson and other non-Christian philosophers saw, this *agape* is a fact of experience and is the most sublime form of love.[56] Hence one can say without exaggeration: if a philosophy of love fails to do justice to *agape*, this amounts to its condemnation as an adequate philosophical conception of the general essence of love.

Let us answer first that the notion of value response is not at all clearly conceived by Nygren. Motivation by values is seen by Nygren in the light of the Platonic conception of *eros*, namely, as an interest in the values of the beloved as a source of my own happiness, of my own satisfaction.[57] This self-centered character is ascribed by Nygren to value response as such. Then it is of course perfectly correct to say that *agape* is not a value response (in this sense). But under this assumed theory of value response we believe that even *eros*, understood here in the sense of natural love between friends, spouses, relatives, etc., is not a "value response." For love in all these forms implies precisely a break-through out of a totally egocentric attitude. Love is

56 See Henri Bergson, *Les deux sources de la Morale et de la Religion.*
57 See Nygren, *Eros und Agape.*

a response to another being because of that being's intrinsic preciousness. Value response in this sense means a response due to another being. In a value response in this sense I do not approach the other person exclusively or primarily as a source of my own happiness, but in a selfless way, as Wojtyła and Styczeń formulate.[58] It must be granted to Nygren that we find much confusion on this point in the philosophy of St. Augustine, St. Thomas Aquinas, and already in Plato and Aristotle.

We have also to welcome Nygren's positive intention (which recalls Fénelon's philosophy of the *amour pur* and his rejection of Bossuet's eudemonism), namely, the intention to gain room for a love "for the beloved's sake."

Yet Nygren precisely fails to see that exclusively value response in the specified sense allows this transcendence of love "for the other's sake." Precisely the most pure value-responding love of God views Him as infinitely good, holy, and beautiful in Himself, and praises and glorifies Him "because of His great glory." *Agape*, here, is unselfish, not because it is unmotivated, or unmotivated by value-preciousness, but precisely because it is motivated by the indwelling preciousness and goodness of the beloved God, to whom all love and honor is due for no other reason than for His intrinsic holiness and goodness.

Furthermore, Nygren fails by confusing two completely different sets of distinctions: the distinction between various categories or types of love, on the one hand, and the distinction between natural love (*eros*) and supernatural love (*agape*), on the other hand. Thus he identifies categorical structures of the divine love for men

---

58   See Wojtyła et al., *Der Streit um den Menschen*, 117–28, 142–51.

or of the Christian love of neighbor with the essence of *agape*, without seeing that *agape* in the form in which it is found in the category of (man's) love of God is the most pure value response. Nygren not only fails to see this but denies it.[59] This criticism should not let us overlook a point which Nygren sees but which his lack of distinctions does not allow him to state unambiguously. It is, namely, truly very hard to see how the merciful love God has for sinners, how the love Christian saints have for their enemies, or the love parents have even for unworthy children, can be called "value response."

We propose the following reply to this objection. Obviously, even in the cited examples the objective value of the beloved person is presupposed. A dog or stone could never be loved in this manner because they lack the intrinsic nobility of the human being as person.

Nygren also overlooks a very profound feature of love which Scheler has stressed to the point of exaggerating it: when, and only when, love has as its object a contingent person in a "pilgrim status" (a *hominem viatorem*), when love is directed to a person in an unfinished state of being, love does not exclusively respond to the actual being of the beloved person. (At least only then is this true in the sense described; it may be the case that—because no finite person can realize all his possibilities and potentialities—the feature of love to be described in a moment belongs to all love for creatures in some sense.) Love sees and embraces also the true vocation of the beloved person: it loves the other also in the light of a beauty which is not yet real in him. It is a special gift which we receive when we are loved, and this gift precisely contains the attitude

---

59   Nygren, *Eros und Agape*, 210ff., 217, 618ff., 678ff.

of the loving person who does not identify us with our faults, who does not "nail us down" to the factual state of our being. Scheler, following Plato, says that in love one always perceives directedness toward higher values than the ones which are already realized. Love is thus visionary, filled with a hope for what is nobler, and creative in helping the beloved person to realize more and more fully this higher form of existence. And as Marcel insists, love is prophetic in asserting and announcing the future reality of this more perfect state and even of immortality.

The vision of the true self which is different from the merely factual self of the beloved person has to be distinguished, however, from arbitrary images which we tend to form of other persons, and which we then project onto the other persons from the outside, as it were. Of course, also persons who truly love others (parents, friends, spouses) often have such self-made images and do violence to the beloved persons by forcing them into such inadequate "molds" or by expecting from them that they adapt to those false "models."

The true vision of the beloved person, proper to love, however, is not such a distorted image. It is rather a faint reflection of part of the meaning of Augustine's statement that God is more interior to ourselves than we ourselves are. The "true self" perceived in love is in one sense already in the beloved person, is even in his most interior being; in another sense, it is not yet actually realized but only anticipated and hoped for.

Scheler emphasizes this movement-character of love so much that he does not want to concede that love is a value response.[60] I do not think, however, that the

60   See Scheler, *Wesen und Formen der Sympathie*, 156–7, 162.

element of movement towards, or care for, the not yet actualized self of the other person makes love less a value response. On the contrary, one could say that love is so much a value response that it does not only respond to the already existing preciousness of the beloved but also to that self which will be hopefully realized in the future and the beauty of which the loving person both sees and affirms. Thus Nygren's correct observation that unworthy and evil persons can be loved does not contradict, but only modifies the value-responding character of love. It leads us to understand the value-response character of love in a deeper sense, which modifies the concept of value response inasmuch as it adds the visionary and creative element which love possesses in relation to the unrealized dimensions of the beloved person's being. It cannot, however, be denied that also that which is only a possibility and a vocation is both discovered and responded to by the loving person. Nonetheless, the phrase "value response" ought to be complemented by other terms such as movement, prophetic character, and creative dimension of love.

One should of course not fail to point out that this directedness of love to the true "non-empirical" self of the beloved person gives occasion to many faults if the lover either forces the other person to become his "true self," without respecting his freedom, or if he confuses self-made images or a superficial understanding of the other with that person's true self. Many of these errors go back to a misunderstanding of the truth about God and man. For, as Wojtyła often elaborates, the true respect and love of man is only possible on the basis of the truth. Man's whole action and being rests on the truth. But the "true self" hidden in each person is also a great mystery of each individual, and no man should pretend too easily to understand it or to have even a limited grasp of it. More important still is the observation that the degree of reality of the true self which is presupposed for love varies greatly depending on the category of love. In parental love or love of neighbor the mere promise or hope that this true self will one day be realized is sufficient for a valid and justified love. In friendship or spousal love it would be dangerous and, in the full sense, even impossible to base such a love on the mere vision of a "true self" if this true self has not yet any reality. There is of course a great difference here between the case where this "true self" is largely unknown and lacks only in reality (such as in the small child) and the case where a caricature of this true self is real in a person in virtue of his meanness and evilness. It is certainly impossible to love someone with the love of friendship or with spousal love if for either of these two reasons the given person's true self is completely unactualized. On the other hand, it is quite possible (for example, in the case of Prince Myshkin's love for Nastassya Filipovna in Dostoyevsky's *The Idiot*) to love someone with spousal love if the reality of this "true self" is only very partially realized.

In other cases of love, such as in the adoring love of God, however, the full reality and realization of the beloved person's being and value is presupposed.

We have to grant Nygren another important point. The thesis that all love is value response must not be identified with the assertion that love cannot go beyond what is deserved by the beloved person. In fact, the only love in which it is absolutely not the case that love gives more than what is deserved is the love of the absolute Being. In the love for any other being and any finite good, and thus certainly in the love for any human contingent person (afflicted with frailty and evils as man is), we find a kind of "paradox of love" in this regard, a strange mixture of apparently opposing elements: of falling short of the response due to the beloved being (the man who truly loves will always think that he does not love enough, if he is not conceited), and of a gift which goes beyond what is strictly speaking "deserved" by the beloved person. The first element is primarily experienced by the person who loves, the second by the one who is loved. This experiential paradox corresponds to a deeper "objective" paradox in the ontological structure of love itself. On the one hand it is true what Polish personalists, especially Styczeń and A. Szostek (following the lead of Wojtyła's philosophical anthropology and ethics), assert: love is the only manner in which the person can be affirmed in the manner proper to him/her. Any response short of love fails to adequately relate to the person as a whole in his/her preciousness so that the person could even be defined as a being which can be affirmed properly solely in love. On the other hand, love contains a self-donation and a total sharing of one's own being which is derived from the whole wealth of a person's being and which is—at least in intention—never confined to what is deserved by the other person but wishes to give much more than what is strictly speaking demanded in justice. In this sense, love gives always more than is deserved and could—in this regard—almost be defined as a response which is not deserved by a person but contains a free gift which exceeds anything deserved.

Moreover, the inner superabundant goodness of love, the free giving beyond what is deserved by the beloved person, characterizes most of all the merciful *agape* with which God loves man and with which we should love every neighbor, regardless how evil and how ferocious an enemy he may be. Yet this love is ultimately only possible because of *agape* in the form of love of God (God's self-love or man's love of God), which is purest value response and never more than what is deserved.

Can love be a response to another person for her own sake if it always seeks requital of love?

Perhaps the deepest and most radical objection against our position is the following, which is in a sense the opposite of Nygren's point: how could we love a person for what he is in himself rather than loving him only for the sake of the strengthening, happiness, fulfillment of our own being? Who would continue to love a person who does not requite our love and give us something in return for our love? Who would continue to love if not only no good came to him through his love but if even sorrow and unending suffering resulted for him from his love? Not because of any selfishness but simply because of the essence of human nature which seeks its own happiness as its primary end, the theory of love as value response appears idealistic, false, and simply untenable. Plato, Aristotle, Augustine, Thomas Aquinas, and many other great thinkers would argue along these lines, even if the pure love tradition lives in these authors themselves (think only of Plato's *Republic II*) and in Duns Scotus, Fénelon, and others.

We cannot sufficiently answer this objection or even unfold the objecting position fully. Yet an attempt must be made to offer at least a short reply to the fundamental question at stake.

Of course, our nature is such that it tends towards fulfillment and happiness. Man wants to become happy. Nygren seems to identify this in a certain rigorist way with egocentricity and selfishness. It is likewise true that we have many tendencies in our nature which coexist with love and which simply aim at an immanent fulfillment of our appetites and of our nature. Nor can it be denied that we desire union with the beloved person and the requital of our love, and that the beloved being and our union with him is the source of greatest personal happiness for us. It has also to be conceded to the objector that man possesses a deep longing for love, and for someone to whom he can be united in love. All of these important facts could easily persuade a thinker that love is basically motivated by the desire for happiness.

Yet there are three decisive facts to keep in mind. In the first place, the coexistence between different relations of a thing to one and the same other being never allows us any identification of these relations. If a man is both humble and proud in his relation to the same other man, we cannot conclude from this that humility is pride. We must also not conclude that to love a person only means to desire this person as fulfillment of our own being because no person loves who does not, if his love is requited and if he sees the other person happy, also rejoice in the beloved being as a source of his own happiness and as fulfillment of his nature. Likewise the coexistence of feeling sheltered by the other and of needing him to spiritually survive does not imply in the least that love is nothing but what coexists with it.

Secondly, there is a deeper sense of fulfillment of the desire to love and a deeper level of happiness in love which precisely presupposes that we take the beloved person seriously in himself. Man is so profoundly ordained towards losing himself, towards surrendering to beings endowed with intrinsic value, that he will never become happy except when he conforms to beings not for his sake only but for their sake. Already Augustine's analysis of the joy in the truth expresses this transcendent dimension of true happiness. The philosophy of love and philosophical anthropology of Wojtyła, von Hildebrand, Styczeń, and others expresses this profound fact that only a "losing of one's life (soul)" for the sake of the beloved person can lead to "gaining one's life (soul)" and that, in fact, the primary motive of this losing must be the other person for his own sake and not the superabundant result of "gaining."

Also the objective ordination of our being to another being is not always for our (the subject's) sake. It can also be an ordination for the sake of the being to which we are ordained. And while it is quite possible that the happiness which accrues superabundantly to us when we love another person for his own sake also co-motivates our love and our interest in the other person, this never allows us to consider our happiness as the primary motive for love. It can neither temporally nor logically-ontologically be the first motive for authentic love. Rather, true love always requires that we know another person as intrinsically good and precious and that the loving person has the center of his life and interest outside of himself, in the beloved person, as Vladimir Solovyov puts it in his book *The Meaning of Love*:

"The meaning and worth of love, as a feeling, is that it really forces us, with all our being, to acknowledge for ANOTHER the same absolute central significance which, because of the power of our egoism, we are conscious of only in our own selves. Love is important not as one of our feelings, but as the transfer of all our interest in life from ourselves to another, as the shifting of the very centre of our personal life. This is characteristic of every kind of love, but predominantly of sexual love; it is distinguished from other kinds of love by greater intensity, by a more engrossing character, and by the possibility of a more complete overall reciprocity. Only this love can lead to the real and indissoluble union of two lives into one."[61] True love always involves that we give our own being, that we give ourselves to the beloved being for his sake. This is not merely psychologically true but also metaphysically. The due-relation as well as the act of self-donation is of metaphysical and anthropological significance. It is characteristic of the person qua person that, while his self-possession and free autonomy is his inalienable possession, he can also freely give himself and not only something possessed by him. And while this self-donation exceeds all other value responses, it also fulfills the very gesture of all true value responses in their transcendent nature.

The capacity to love, to take interest in a person because this person calls for a response in virtue of his indwelling preciousness, belongs to the deepest characteristics of man, of the person. Likewise, to be the proper object-person to be affirmed in love elucidates the metaphysical essence of the person and expresses it simultaneously because it reflects the intrinsic and unique value proper to the person. The capacity to love in this sense belongs to the *raison d'être* of man, of the universe, of being itself.

---

61 Vladimir Solovyov, *The Meaning of Love*. Introd. by Owen Barfield. ransl. Jane Marshall (1946). Ed. and sbstantially revised translation by Thomas R. Beyer, Jr. (West Stockbridge, MA: Inner Traditions Lindies Farne Press, 1985), ch. 3. p. 51.

INDEX

About Love (Pieper), 40
The Acting Person
    (Wojtyła), 39
agape, ix, 10, 43–46, 50
amour pur, 45
Annonce Faite à Marie
    (Claudel), 32
antiphon, 19
Aquinas, Thomas (saint).
    See St. Thomas Aquinas
Aristotle, 7, 11–14, 16, 25,
    45, 51
attractiveness, 9. *See also*
    sexual attractiveness
Augustine. *See* St.
    Augustine
authentic love, 36, 53

Beatrice (character in
    Divine Comedy), 39
beauty: becoming trans-
    parent of, 18–19; gifts
    of, 17–18; illusion of
    non-existent beauty, 35;
    perception of, 34–35;
    priority of love over, 36
beloved being/beloved
    person, 2–4, 7, 9–10,
12, 14–16, 18–19, 21,
    26, 28, 30, 32–35, 36,
    37–38, 40–42, 46–50,
    52–53
Bergson, Henri, 44
bestowed dignity, 20
bonum mihi, 11–12
bonum tibi, 11–12
Bossuet, Jacques-Bénigne,
    45

categorical imperative, 2–
    3n3, 6
child, love of, 18, 26, 32, 42
Claudel, Paul, 32
Cordelia (character in *King*
    Lear), 38–39
credit, as gift of genuine
    love, 35–36

Dante, Alighieri, 39
data, called love, 9
demonic person, 20, 26
dignity, 3–4, 14, 18n20, 19–
    21, 26, 32, 37
Divine Comedy (Dante), 39
divine love, 44–45
Don Giovanni, 1–3, 7

Dostoyevsky, Fyodor, 33, 49

due-relation, 15n18, 54

Eigenleben (personal life), 12

enemy, love of, 33

eros, 10, 43–45

esse (existence), 42

essence and existence, 41

eudaimonia (happiness), 11

eudemonism, 45

Ezekiel 28:12–17, 27n30

Faust (Goethe), 35

Fénelon, François, 45, 51

Frankfurt, Harry, x–xi

Frankl, Viktor, 9

freedom, 4, 17–18, 20, 22, 26, 28, 48

Freud, Sigmund, 35

friendship, 4, 12, 18, 33, 49

gaining one's life (soul), 53

genuine love, 1, 4–5, 36

gifts, 17–19, 21–26, 35, 46, 50

God, love of, 9, 21, 49, 51

Goethe, Johann Wolfgang von, 34–35

grace, 26n29

happiness: according to Aristotle, 11; desire for, 35; as end and ultimate motive of all actions, 13; forms of, 5; love as motivated by desire for, 52; as not first motive for authentic love, 53; as secondary motivating factor, 14 transcendent dimension of, 53; true happiness, 8

Hartmann, N., 38

hedonistic approach (to other persons)/hedonism, 7–8

hedonistic-utilitarian ideal/principle (of the good), 7–8

Hobbes, Thomas, 8n9

Hoffmann, E. T. A., 35

hominem viatorem (pilgrim status), 46

The Idiot (Dostoyevsky), 33, 49

imaginary preciousness, 35

imperfect man, love of, 9

individuellen Kern der Dinge, auf den Wertkern ("to the value-core of things and persons"), 16

Ingarden, Roman, 31

integration, 10
intrinsic importance, 2–3
intrinsic preciousness, 2, 3, 12, 25, 29, 39, 45
intrinsic value, 4–5n6, 12–13, 30, 38, 53, 54
intrinsic worth, 11

John Paul II (pope). *See* Wojtyła, Karol

Kant, Immanuel, 2, 6
Kater Murr (Hoffmann), 35
King Lear (Shakespeare), 38–39
knowledge, relationship of to love, 34

Le Petit Prince (Saint Expuéry), 37
Leonardo da Vinci, 18
Liebe, 10
losing of one's life (soul), 53
love: authentic love, 36, 53; basic unity of meaning in term, 10; capacity to, 54; of child, 18, 26, 32, 42; as differing from value response, 15; divine love, 44–45; of enemy, 33; genuine love, 1, 4–5, 36; of God, 9, 21, 49, 51; in love, 31; as more than a value response, 24; movement-character of, 47; of neighbor, 19, 21, 33, 46, 49; as not sufficiently characterized as value response, 16, 39; paradox of, 50; parental love, 19, 49; as prophetic, 47; pseudo-love, 3, 5, 9; real love, 9, 39; relationship of knowledge to, 34; response of, 21; as response to a being (person), 28; as response to other person as whole, 25; role of in education and improvement of person, 36–37; spousal love, 10, 18, 21, 22–25, 31–33, 49; true love, 35–36, 53–54; as value response, 9–11, 14, 24, 27–28, 40, 42, 48–49; value-responding character of, 34, 48; as visionary, 47; of wine, 1–3, 5, 9; of women, 1–3, 5

Love and Responsibility
    (Wojtyła), 7, 21–22
loveableness, 21n21, 26, 40

Marcel, Gabriel, 21n22, 28,
    47
The Meaning of Love
    (Volovyov), 53
Measure for Measure
    (Shakespeare), 43
The Merchant of Venice
    (Shakespeare), 43
moral dignity, 20
moral evil, 20
moral goodness, 17, 20,
    25–27

natural endowments, 26
neighbor, love of, 19, 21,
    33, 46, 49
Nietzsche, Friedrich, 35
Nygren, Anders, 10, 43–46,
    48–49, 51

objective good for the per-
    son, 11, 12
objective value, 11, 46
over-value response, 14

paradox of love, 50
parental love, 19, 49
Pascal, Blaise, 34

perfectio perfectionum (per-
    fection of all perfec-
    tions), 38
person qua person, 16, 20,
    54
*persona est affirmanda
    propter seipsam*, 4
personalistic principle, 6
persons: attitudes toward
    as confused with love,
    6; using of, 6
philosophical anthropolo-
    gy, 10
Pieper, Josef, 10, 25, 31–32,
    38, 40
Plato, 14, 45, 47, 51
Platonists, 38, 44
pleasure, compared to
    happiness, 8
Polish personalists, 50
Portia (character in *The
    Merchant of Venice*), 43
preciousness, 2, 8, 14, 16,
    19–21, 28, 32–33, 37–39,
    41, 43, 45, 48, 50, 54
principles of being, 40
pseudo-love, 3, 5, 9

real love, 9, 39
The Reasons of Love
    (Frankfurt), x
Republic II (Plato), 51

Rickert, Heinrich, 38
Roberts, Mark, 29–30

Saint Exupéry, Antoine de, 37
Scheler, Max, 9, 16, 25, 29–32, 34, 37–38, 42, 46–47
Scotus, Duns, 14, 51
se jouir de, 8
secondary motives, 14
self-centered pleasure, 5
self-donation, 21–22, 24, 50, 54
sex, pseudo-love for, 5, 9
sexual attractiveness, 1, 10, 35
sexual relations, 7
Shakespeare, William, 39, 43
spousal love, 10, 18, 21–25, 31–33, 49
St. Augustine, 34, 45, 47, 51, 53
St. Beda the Priest, 42n53
St. Thomas Aquinas, 14, 38, 45, 51
Styczeń, Tadeusz, 4, 45, 50, 53
Symposium (Plato), 14
Szostek, A., 50

Thomists, 37–38, 40, 42

true love, 35–36, 53–54
true self, 36, 47–49

utilitarian approach (to love)/utilitarianism, 6–8
uzywaz, 8

value, as elaborated by von Hildebrand, 2
value response, 4–5n, 9, 10–11, 14–16, 24, 27–32, 40, 42, 44–46, 48–49
value-eide, 38–39
value-ideas, 38
value-preciousness, 12–14, 29, 45
value-properties, 19
value-qualities, 31
value-radiance, 16
Volovyov, Vladimir, 53
von Hildebrand, Dietrich, 2, 9, 11–12, 19, 21, 29, 30, 34, 53

wine, love of, 1–3, 5, 9
Wohlwollen (benevolence), 13
Wojtyła, Karol, 2, 4, 6–8, 10, 21, 39–40, 45, 48, 50, 53
women: love of, 1–3, 5; taking advantage of, 8